backstage _pass_

Backstage at a
MOVIE SET

Katherine Wessling

HIGH
interest
books

Children's Press®
A Division of Scholastic Inc.
New York / Toronto / London / Auckland / Sydney
Mexico City / New Delhi / Hong Kong
Danbury, Connecticut

Thank you to the cast and crew of Riding Shotgun. *Special thanks to the film's director J.M. Finholt.*

Book Design: Daniel Hosek and Chris Logan
Contributing Editor: Matthew Pitt

Photo Credits: Cover, p. 23 © John Barrett/Globe Photos Inc.; p. 4 © Lucasfilm Ltd./Everett Collection; pp. 7, 19, 24, 26, 28, 31, 32, 35 J.M. Finholt; p. 8 U.S. Department of the Interior, National Park Service, Edison National Historic Site; p. 11 © Robert Landau/Corbis; p. 12 © Bettmann/Corbis; p. 15 © Warner Bros./Everett Collection; pp. 16, 20 © Mitchell Gerber/Corbis; p. 36 Cory Foster; p. 38 © Columbia Pictures/courtesy Everett Collection; p. 40 Rosen Publishing

Library of Congress Cataloging-in-Publication Data

Wessling, Katherine.
  Backstage at a movie set / Katherine Wessling.
  p. cm.—(Backstage pass)
  Summary: Explores the history of motion picture production, key players in the process of making a film, a typical day of shooting, and how to pursue one's interest in the field, either as a career or as a hobby.
  ISBN 0-516-24325-X (lib. bdg.) ISBN 0-516-24387-X (pbk.)
  1. Cinematography—Juvenile literature. 2. Motion pictures—Production and direction—Juvenile literature. [1. Cinematography. 2. Motion pictures—Production and direction.] I. Title. II. Series.

TR851 .W47 2003
791.43'023—dc21
                                                        2002008597

CONTENTS

Introduction 5

1 The Wonderful World
of Movies 9

2 Ready for Action 17

3 We're Rolling! 25

4 Breaking In 39

New Words 42

For Further Reading 44

Resources 45

Index 47

About the Author 48

To make audiences believe in the lightsaber duels and Jedi magic of *Star Wars*, director George Lucas had to pull off some sorcery of his own.

Introduction

The house lights dim. Giant speakers swell with sound. People in the packed audience stop chattering. All eyes focus on the screen at the front of the movie theater. Instantly, the hushed crowd is transported to another time and place. Darth Maul leaps across the screen. He's attacking two Jedi knights with his dual-sided lightsaber. If he defeats these brave Jedis, there's no telling what damage he could do. Queen Amidala could be killed. The galaxy might even fall into the hands of the Empire.

The audience knows that what they are seeing on-screen is fiction. Yet movies have the power to bring fantasies to life. Movies entertain us with tales of romance, adventure, and human triumph. They dazzle us with special effects and lush soundtracks.

Sometimes we're so mesmerized by a film that time seems to slip away. You may not want to leave the theater, even after the last scene fades to black. Have you ever stayed seated long enough to watch the film's credits roll? The list of names and jobs is overwhelming. It takes hundreds of creative people to make one motion picture. This crew often works under difficult conditions. They must play their different roles to perfection. To complete the film on time, they must follow a grueling schedule. In the end, though, all the hard work pays off.

Do you want to learn how the magic is created? Would you like to become part of the film crew that makes this magic, dazzling moviegoers across the nation? Want to get a taste of what being on a film set is like? Well, turn the page, and let's get rolling!

While a film's cast says their lines, hundreds of talented artists behind the camera are busy performing other important roles.

One early film shown in Kinetoscope parlors was called *Fred Ott's Sneeze*. Featuring an employee of Edison's who made a silly sneeze for the camera, it was one of the first hit films.

CHAPTER ONE

The Wonderful World of Movies

Movies have captured peoples' imaginations for generations. Yet just over a hundred years ago, there *were* no movies. In 1889, inventor Thomas Alva Edison changed that. Edison and his assistant, William Kennedy Laurie Dickson, developed a machine called the Kinetoscope. Inside a Kinetoscope, strips of still photographs moved from one spool to another. Viewers looked through a small peephole in the machine. As they did, the still images appeared to move. The viewers were rewarded with a dazzling 30-second film.

In 1894, Kinetoscope parlors opened in several cities. Each parlor had two rows of Kinetoscopes. Since a Kinetoscope cost a nickel to use, the parlors became known as "nickelodeons." The short movies featured popular performers of the time. For example, one film showed famous bodybuilder Eugen Sandow flexing his muscles.

Kinetoscopes were a hit across the world. Two French brothers, Louis and Auguste Lumière, improved on Edison's machine. They developed a device that could take pictures as well as project them onto a screen. The Lumières shot their first black-and-white film in 1895.

LOCATION, LOCATION, LOCATION

It's hard not to mention Hollywood when speaking of films. After all, Hollywood, California, is home to many major motion picture studios. This, however, wasn't always the case. In the early days of film, American movies were made mostly in New York City or New Jersey.

So why did filmmakers go west? Hollywood's great weather made shooting movies all year long possible. Also, the terrain in southern California features many different kinds of scenery. There are mountains, oceans, deserts, and forests. This variety gave filmmakers many choices for settings.

Sometimes, only small bits of films are actually shot in the towns they're set in. Let's say a film is set in St. Louis, Missouri. The camera crew might

Once filmmakers saw the benefits of the sunny southern California weather, they were yelling, "Hooray for Hollywood!"

travel to St. Louis for one day. There, they could shoot footage of major landmarks, such as the Arch. The rest of the film, however, might be shot on a Hollywood movie set made to look like St. Louis. Hollywood set designers are experts at recreating cities and towns from all over the world.

BREAKING THE SILENCE

Until the late 1920s, all movies were silent. They had no sound. Often, words the characters spoke were printed on-screen for the audience to read. Theater owners knew that sound enhanced the pleasures of viewing films. So musicians were

Hit films, such as *The Jazz Singer*, featured soundtracks that really grabbed their audiences' ears.

often hired to accompany the on-screen action. For instance, suppose the villain of a silent film kidnaps a woman and ties her to railroad tracks. As an oncoming train approached, a pianist might start playing dark, ominous notes. When the movie's hero rescued the woman, the music might become livelier. Smaller theaters were only able to afford a pianist. The larger theaters, though, sometimes featured a full orchestra!

In 1927, Warner Brothers Studios produced *The Jazz Singer*. This was the first popular movie to have a soundtrack. A soundtrack is a sound recording that runs along with the pictures. Audiences could now hear their favorite actors talking and singing.

ART FOR ALL

As the century rolled forward, movies made a deeper mark on our culture. Whether audiences wanted to watch romances blooming, action unfolding, or slapstick humor, movies provided the pleasures. What's more, this entertainment was affordable. People loved other performing arts, such as plays and classical music. Many families, however, didn't earn enough money to enjoy these leisure activities. Movies provided an inexpensive way to experience the magic of performance.

People turned to movies for relaxation and information as well as entertainment. In fact, a day at the movies once lasted for several hours. It included a double feature (two movies), a newsreel, a cartoon, and previews of coming attractions.

CAUSE AND EFFECTS

The look of movies has changed over the years. One big breakthrough was the introduction of color. Thanks to color technology, films looked more vivid than ever. By the 1960s, almost all motion pictures were shot in color, instead of black and white.

Advances in special effects also enhanced films greatly. Simple special effects had always been a part of early movies. In 1977, however, they were taken to a whole new level. The movie *Star Wars* hit the big screen and awed crowds. Audiences were dazzled by shots of hovering landspeeders and dueling lightsabers.

Before *Star Wars*, movie studios did not have special-effects facilities. To achieve those effects, director George Lucas had to create his own company, Industrial Light and Magic (ILM). Since then, ILM's brilliant effects have been used in hundreds of films, from *The Mask* to *The Mummy*.

Thanks to ILM, *The Perfect Storm* was able to bring wave after wave of special effects into viewers' laps.

A great director allows his or her cast and crew to give their creative input. As this photo shows, however, directors always remain in the driver's seat.

CHAPTER TWO

Ready for Action

Filmmaking involves hundreds of talented people. Each person's work is guided by the same basic plan—the screenplay. A screenplay, or script, contains a film's plot, character actions, and character dialogue. Screenwriters often create screenplays for movies based on their own ideas. These works are called original screenplays. Other times, screenwriters base their scripts on a book or story that has already been published. These scripts are called adapted screenplays.

LENS CRAFTERS

Directors oversee the process of bringing screenplays to the big screen. They sculpt each film's look, feel, and sound. They decide from what camera angles to shoot, or film, a movie's scenes. They give their cast of actors guidance and advice about playing the characters.

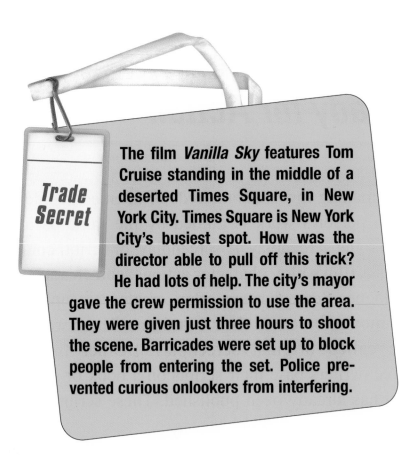

Trade Secret

The film *Vanilla Sky* features Tom Cruise standing in the middle of a deserted Times Square, in New York City. Times Square is New York City's busiest spot. How was the director able to pull off this trick? He had lots of help. The city's mayor gave the crew permission to use the area. They were given just three hours to shoot the scene. Barricades were set up to block people from entering the set. Police prevented curious onlookers from interfering.

Of course, no director can do everything alone. They work with cinematographers each step of the way. Cinematographers help directors figure out the best way to shoot a movie. They also help decide what locations to use for shooting.

A film's director and cinematographer also collaborate, or work together, on lighting each scene. Perfect lighting helps set a movie's mood. Perhaps a character is running for his life from the

film's villain. The crew may cast the villain in shad-
ows to play up his evil nature. They may shine harsh
lights close to the victim's face to indicate his fear.

Even before the first scenes are shot, directors
are hard at work preparing to film their movies.
One of the first things directors prepare is a breakdown script. The breakdown details every scene in

Filmmakers set up their lighting equipment with great
care, thought, and precision. Lighting techniques help
add to the mood of a film.

the script. It breaks each scene into separate shots. For each shot, the camera will be placed at a different angle to capture another aspect of the scene.

ACTING OUT

Directors also decide which actors they want in their casts. To a movie audience, great actors always seem perfect for the parts they play. Actors must research their characters and memorize the

Directors cast background actors for many reasons. In this scene, the presence of background actors amplifies an already tense scene.

script's dialogue. They read their scripts over and over. They may even ask questions along the way: What is my character feeling as she says this line? What kind of relationship does she have to other characters? The stars of films are called lead actors. Denzel Washington and Julia Roberts are examples of current lead actors.

Of course, most cast members aren't lead actors. Each film usually has several supporting actors. While these actors don't appear in every scene, they still have crucial roles. Even actors who don't have any lines are hired. These performers are known as extras, or background actors.

Any actor who wants to be cast in a movie usually auditions for the role. In an audition, a director asks actors to read dialogue from the screenplay. The director sometimes auditions two lead actors at once, to see whether they have good chemistry. For instance, if two actors are supposed to be in love, there should be a spark between them. If the audition goes well, the actors will often do a screen test. This means the cinematographer will film them performing a scene from the screenplay.

Once the movie is cast, rehearsals begin. The actors and director meet to read and discuss the script. With the director's help, actors start bringing life to their characters. They ask the director questions about their characters. The director encourages them to experiment with different readings and gestures.

WE'RE ALL SET

Of course, most people hired to work on a film never show up on-screen. These skilled, dedicated crew members work behind the scenes. One of these is the art director, who designs the sets. An art director skillfully replicated the Statue of Liberty for the hit film *X-Men*. On this set, Professor X's band of heroes fought, and defeated, Magneto. Other crew members are in charge of makeup and hairdressing. They are the ones who supplied the lightning bolt scar on Harry Potter's forehead. Costume supervisors choose the actors' wardrobes. For instance, they keep Mike Myers looking like a 1960s-era British spy in the Austin Powers films.

Preparation for a film often takes months. All this preparation will help a film shoot go smoothly.

The person most responsible for keeping a film running on time and under budget is the producer. Producers hire all the necessary crew members. They help each person get his or her job done. Producers make sure everyone is ready to roll when the director yells, "Action!"

Makeup artists never fail to bring out the best side of film stars, such as Jennifer Lopez.

Practice makes perfect: Actors playing the brothers in *Broad Daylight* rehearse their lines. Since shooting a scene is so expensive, actors know they must be ready to go before the camera rolls.

CHAPTER THREE

We're Rolling!

Today is the first day of shooting for the movie *Broad Daylight*. This film is an action-packed tale of suspense. It's the story of three brothers on a desperate search for their missing father. The film's budget is $20 million. That sounds like a lot, but it's actually a modest budget for a major motion picture. The crew is under pressure to stay within that budget.

6:00 A.M.

Filming often begins at the crack of dawn, especially for outdoor shoots. Starting near sunrise allows the cinematographer to make the best use of natural light. There are also fewer distractions, such as automobile traffic and curious onlookers.

The *Broad Daylight* crew springs into action at their first location, an abandoned alley. The assistant director, or AD, is already there to pass along

Did somebody say "Action!"? Film crews are often unloading equipment and taking care of dozens of details at sunrise, while most of their friends are home sleeping.

key instructions from the director. The AD helps the director keep on schedule. The crew has many things to do before the actors arrive. They must set up cameras, lights, and sound-recording devices. This huge, heavy equipment often fills several trucks.

Each cast and crew member carries a call sheet with them. Call sheets are schedules that indicate the time everyone must appear on the set. They also detail what scenes will be shot during the day.

Trade Secret

Filmmakers try to make a profit on their movies. However, box-office flops happen all too often. The biggest blunder ever was the 2001 film *Town and Country*. This ill-fated flick cost $85 million to make. Yet it made less than $7 million. Other big-screen bombs include *Cutthroat Island* (1995) and *Heaven's Gate* (1981).

After a day's shooting is wrapped, or completed, call sheets for the next day are passed out. Often a shoot will last from dawn through dusk. Luckily, each set features a craft services table, which provides plenty to eat and drink. This way, the cast and crew don't have to leave the set when they get thirsty or hungry.

7:00 A.M.

It's call time for the actors who play the three brothers. They head to their mobile dressing rooms, or trailers. There, they have their hair and makeup done and change into costumes. By 8:30 A.M., everyone is ready to shoot scene 1. The action will go like this:

The brothers are sleeping in their bedrooms. Suddenly, they're awakened by the sound of tires squealing on the driveway. They rush to the front door and glimpse a man shoving their father into a car.

Before each take, the clapboard is placed in front of the camera and filmed. This way, crew members reviewing the footage will know what scene and take of the film they are watching.

The oldest brother gets a look at the getaway car. The youngest brother picks up a comb he sees lying on the driveway.

Scene 1 begins at sunrise. The actors are nervous because this is their first scene in the film. The director keeps them calm and relaxed. Then the director and cinematographer go over the blocking, or movements, they want the actors to make in the scene. Each movement is carefully planned and marked on the ground with tape. The actors must "hit," or stand on, these marks.

8:30 A.M.

It's time to shoot. The AD yells, "Quiet on the set!" Once everyone quiets down, she yells, "Roll it!" Other crew members bark out shorthand phrases of their own. These phrases let the whole set know when each key player is ready to begin. The sound engineer says, "Speed," once the sound recording begins. The camera operator yells, "Rolling!" the instant the camera starts to film. An assistant camera operator walks to the camera with a clapboard. Written on this clapboard is the number of the scene being shot and the take number. A take refers to each attempt to shoot a scene. The assistant says, "Scene one, take one." Then he claps the clapboard in front of the camera.

Finally, the director yells, "Action!" Halfway through the scene, one actor says the wrong line. The actor playing the youngest brother giggles. "Cut!" yells the director. People rush in to touch up the actors' makeup. The cast and crew must all return "back to one"—the spot where they began the scene. The AD yells for quiet. This time, the clapboard shows, "Scene one, take two."

They don't get far into the scene before the director yells, "Cut!" again. When the actors ask what's wrong, the director points to the boom. The boom is a long pole with a big microphone attached to it. The microphone is held above the camera during film shoots to pick up sound. Unfortunately, the boom operator let the boom drop too far. It showed up in the shot.

Before they can retake the scene, the sun disappears behind a cloud. More lights must be brought in to mimic the bright sunlight. This takes a while, pushing the shoot behind schedule. The director is getting nervous.

This boom operator is holding a highly sensitive microphone. If he fidgets or makes any sound while following the actors, the sound quality will be affected. To reproduce the sound perfectly, he must match the actors step for step.

Finally, they're ready to shoot the third take of scene 1. They shoot the entire scene without interruption. The director yells, "Print it!" This means he wants to keep that shot. Still, they're not quite done filming scene 1. For take four, the director wants to capture the scene from a different camera angle. The cinematographer swivels the camera behind the back of the actor playing the middle brother, James. Now the camera will record the expressions of the actor playing the oldest brother, Sean. This is called an over-the-shoulder shot.

They shoot the scene successfully from this new angle. Now the director wants the actor playing

Directors want to see all their actors shine. The best of them—like the director of *Broad Daylight*—are wonderful at coaching their cast into giving command performances.

Sean to ad-lib. Ad-libs are lines that actors make up on their own. Some directors prefer to stick to the screenplay's dialogue. This director, however, likes to experiment. He knows audiences must believe the brothers have a close relationship. If the actors keep saying the same dialogue over and over, their lines may sound flat, or unemotional. The actor ad-libs a line suggesting that he suspects his father's kidnapper was a family friend.

The director is pleased that they have covered the scene from so many different angles. He is ready to move on.

10:45 A.M.

The director skips ahead to scene 10. Films are often shot out of sequence. The scenes are shot in the order that makes it easiest on the cast and crew. For instance, scene 1 takes place at sunrise. Scene 2, however, takes place at night. Rather than wait for the sun to set, the crew shoots scene 10, which takes place during daylight hours.

In the script, scene 10 takes place the day after scene 1. Therefore, each actor must change into a new costume. The director points out the marks to his actors. In this scene, the brothers speak to a detective named Paula. She's trying to help them find their father. However, she hasn't been able to find any solid clues. They finish the scene after shooting from four different angles. At 1:00 P.M., everyone in the cast and crew breaks for lunch.

2:00 P.M.

Scene 6 is the next to be shot. The producer is a bit worried. It looks like it's going to rain. Also, the shoot is running behind schedule. It has to be finished by 4:00 P.M. That's because the permit allowing the crew to be at this location expires at 5:00 P.M. sharp.

The director and actors run through scene 6. In this scene, Paula meets Sean for the first time. She gets out of her squad car and walks toward him. Just as they finish their blocking, the rain starts. Everyone is stressed. They have to wait until the rain stops.

3:25 P.M.

The weather finally clears. The crew dries off the squad car and returns to their places. The producer reminds everyone that they must finish this shot by 4:00 P.M. The cast and crew cross their fingers, hoping that nothing goes wrong. It doesn't! They finish the scene with no mistakes. The director is beaming as he yells, "That's a wrap!"

It's time to go home. The actors return to their trailers, change clothes, and remove their makeup. The crew wearily packs the equipment into the trucks and cleans the area.

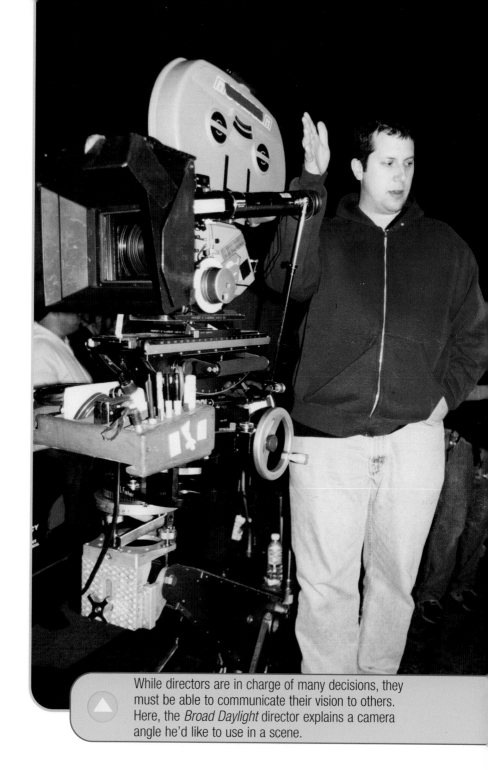

While directors are in charge of many decisions, they must be able to communicate their vision to others. Here, the *Broad Daylight* director explains a camera angle he'd like to use in a scene.

A difficult dolly shot may take hours to prepare and perfect. However, it may only show up on-screen for a single moment.

8:00 P.M.

The producer, the director, and the cinematographer meet to view the footage shot during the day. This footage is called the dailies. They make sure they've captured all the necessary shots. They're thrilled with the footage. The director, however, wishes he had filmed a close-up of Justin, the youngest brother, in scene 10. That's when Justin hears that the police don't have any strong clues. Then he suddenly realizes that the comb he picked up from the driveway may belong to the kidnapper and may help solve the case. The producer and cinematographer suggest filming a pickup of the actor's reaction. A pickup is when filmmakers redo a small part of a scene. The director decides to use a dolly for the shot. Dollies are wheeled platforms that carry cameras. The moving camera will help enhance Justin's surprised reaction.

Finally, at 10 P.M., the crew says goodnight. They accomplished a lot today. However, they have weeks of shooting left. After all, a daylong shoot only provides about 3 minutes of footage in the final film!

Audiences were thrilled by the web-spinning antics seen in *Spider-Man*. However, it was the strong story the director and writer spun that kept viewers glued to their seats.

CHAPTER FOUR

Breaking In

Film sets are hectic, yet rewarding, workplaces. Now that you know how films get produced, maybe you want to do more than just watch them. Do you want to actually become involved in the process? There are dozens of jobs to choose from.

A good way to start putting your dreams in motion is to join your school's drama club. Some schools allow their students to design stage sets and costumes. Students may even be allowed to direct plays.

If acting is in your blood, audition for a small independent film. Just remember that in high school plays, a freshman might get the chance to play a much older character. Films, however, are very age specific. So you should be looking for roles that fit your age.

You could also volunteer as a production assistant (PA) for a local film shoot. This would give you firsthand experience of the different aspects of filmmaking. Production assistants do a lot of hard work, but don't get much credit for it. However, it's

No matter what side of the lens you prefer to stand on, making a fun and successful film can make you feel like a star!

a great way to break into film. Because PAs work all over the set, they get to meet, and impress, many members of the crew. Even the famous director Steven Spielberg had to start somewhere! Spielberg's break came when he was hired as a PA for Universal Studios.

Getting to the top of the film industry is a long climb. For many, that climb starts with learning about their craft in school. That's why many colleges offer courses in filmmaking. These courses teach the basics of filmmaking, from camera filters to sound effects. Of course, if you want to be a filmmaker, you're probably already doing some of your homework—watching movies! You can keep learning each time you watch one. Pay close attention to the actors' performances. Also, study how the story is told and what camera angles are used.

Do you have a video camera? If so, you can experiment with filmmaking. Try to make your movie feel as fun and exciting as your favorite films. Write your own short script with friends. Include a homemade special effect or two. Edit your favorite songs into a soundtrack.

Your first effort may not look as sleek as, say, *Spider-Man*. On the other hand, camera quality is becoming better and prices are getting cheaper all the time. More movies these days are being shot on video instead of film. *The Blair Witch Project* and *Star Wars Episode II: Attack of the Clones* are two recent examples. More than ever, it doesn't take bags of money to finish your first film, or put it "in the can."

Moviemaking will always take lots of hard work and dedication. When you create a film that inspires people and tells a moving story, though, you know your effort has paid off.

auditions try-out performances by actors to see if they are suitable for a part in a film

boom a long pole that has a microphone attached to it

breakdown an extremely detailed list of everything needed to shoot a movie

call sheet a daily schedule for each member of the cast and crew

call time the time each cast and crew member must arrive at the set

cast all of the actors in a movie

crew the team of people on a movie set who work on the film's technical aspects

dailies film footage that has been shot each day

dialogue words spoken by actors

marks the spots that actors must stand on in a scene; often marked with strips of tape

scene a segment of a screenplay that tells one piece of the story

screenplay a movie's script, containing the story, the characters' actions, and the dialogue

screen test a filmed performance by the actors who are being considered for a role

soundtrack the audio portion of a movie

take a scene that is being filmed

Balcziak, Bill, and Mark E. Ahlstrom. *Movies.*
Vero Beach, FL: Rourke Enterprises, Inc., 1989.

Coulter, George and Shirley. *Movies.* Vero Beach,
FL: Rourke Publishing Inc., 1996.

Cross, Robin. *Movie Magic: A Behind-the-Scenes
Look at Filmmaking.* New York: Sterling
Publishing Company, Inc., 1996.

Platt, Richard. *Eyewitness: Film.* New York:
Dorling Kindersley Publishing, Inc., 2000.

Schwartz, Perry. *Making Movies.* Minneapolis,
MN: The Lerner Publishing Group, 1989.

ORGANIZATIONS

Association of Independent Feature Film Producers
P.O. Box 38755
Hollywood, CA 90038
www.aiffp.org
This organization will help you learn more about producing an independent feature film.

Directors Guild of America
Los Angeles Headquarters
7920 Sunset Boulevard
Los Angeles, CA 90046
(800) 421-4173
www.dga.org
Learn more about directing by contacting this guild.

Writers Guild of America
7000 West Third Street
Los Angeles, CA 90048
(800) 548-4532
www.wga.org
On this Web site, you can learn more about screenwriting.

RESOURCES

WEB SITES

Internet Movie Database
www.imdb.com
This site provides plot summaries, cast and crew lists, gossip, and updates of thousands of films, old and new.

Lerner.org
www.learner.org/exhibits/cinema
A great site providing lots of interesting information about moviemaking, including hands-on activities.

The Library of Congress — American Memory
http://lcweb2.loc.gov/ammem/edhtml/edhome.html
This site contains clips from very early films made by Thomas Alva Edison.

Screen Actors Guild
www.sag.org/terminology.html
This site provides a useful glossary of film terms.

A

ad-lib, 32
audition, 21

B

boom, 30
breakdown script, 19
budget, 23, 25

C

call sheet, 26–27
call time, 27
cast, 17, 20, 27, 30,
    33–34
cinematographer, 18, 21,
    25, 29, 31, 37
clapboard, 29–30
crew, 6, 19, 25, 27, 30,
    33–34, 37, 40

D

dailies, 37
dialogue, 17, 21, 32
director, 14, 17–23,
    25–26, 29–34, 37, 40
dolly, 37
drama club, 39

E

Edison, Thomas Alva, 9

H

Hollywood, 10–11

I

Industrial Light and
    Magic (ILM), 14

J

Jazz Singer, The, 12

K

Kinetoscope, 9–10

L

Lumière, Louis and
   Auguste, 10

M

marks, 29, 33

N

nickelodeons, 9

P

production assistant
   (PA), 39–40

S

scene, 5, 17–22, 26,
   28–31, 33–34, 37
screenplay, 17, 21, 32
screen test, 21
script, 17, 19–22, 33, 41
soundtrack, 5, 12, 41

T

take, 29–31

V

volunteer, 39

W

Warner Brothers, 12

About the Author

Katherine Wessling has performed as an actor in movies, including the independent film *Earthen Vessels*. Her writing has appeared in many magazines. She has also been an editor at *Speak*, *Swing*, *performance for the planet*, and *Good Housekeeping*.